The Moral of The Story

A One Act Comedy for Children

by

Valetta Anderson

Published
by
Havescripts

An imprint of Blue Moon Plays

Moral of the Story © 2000 by Valetta Anderson
All rights reserved.

Publisher: Blue Moon Plays, LLC
1385 Fordham Road, Ste 105-279
Virginia Beach, VA 23464
Printed in the USA
Cover Art: Library of Congress, Words to the Wise:
https://read.gov/aesop/index.htm

ISBN: 978-1-943416-94-3

Special Considerations:
Small-group readings around a table or in the classroom:

- If you are planning to use this script FOR CLASSROOM USE, you must purchase scripts for the members of your class or group. These may be purchased as a downloadable PDF (class/group study pack) which may be printed for that class only.
- If you are a small group doing private play readings for YOUR OWN ENTERTAINMENT or for a SMALL SENIOR ACTIVITY GROUP, you must purchase the number or scripts required by the characters: these may be purchased as a multi-copy download which will give you a printable script that you may copy for that reading only.

Video Taping
One video tape may be made for archival purposes only.

Livestreaming
Livestreaming is permissible with an additional fee.

Digital versions cannot be added to a free or paid online library or website, in any format, with or without member access, without the publisher's permission.

TO PERFORM THIS PLAY

<u>You must buy sufficient scripts for the cast + 3, apply for performance rights, pay the performance fee, and receive a performance license.</u>

To purchase scripts:

- Purchase sufficient printed hard copies (one for each cast member, plus 3 for the crew) - an automatic 10 percent discount is applied to multiple printed hardcopies at the point of ordering.

    or

- Purchase a Multicopy PDF which allows you to print sufficient copies of this script (one for each cast member, plus 3 for the crew). Click Return to Merchant to download your printable PDF. A link to the download will also be emailed to you, along with a link to the application for performance license.

To apply for a Performance License, go to the Product Page of the play and fill out and submit the application form.

To pay the Performance Fee, simply pay the invoice you will be emailed when we receive your application for performance.

Your Performance License for your requested dates will be emailed to you.

All scripts and licenses shall be obtained at Blue Moon Plays at www.havescripts.com

If you wish to make changes in the script of any kind, you must receive permission from the publisher or the playwright. Permission is usually granted readily when schools or theaters face casting problems and the changes do not affect the quality or intent of the original.

For information, visit www.havescripts.com;
email info@bluemoonplays.com
or call 757-816-1164

Moral of the Story

About The Play: Why does Harry Hare, television spokes-hare for the National Council on Carrots, race his longtime friend, Tommy Tortoise? And why can't Harry's niece, Harriet Hare, spell carrot? This modernized children's play contains an ancient Ibo (northern Nigeria) legend and reveals what inquiring minds have always wanted to know... the inside scoop behind Aesop's most famous Fable and why tortoises have cracked, lumpy shells.

Time & Place: Present day Hare Town and ancient Iboland.

Set: 1) Harriet Hare's home living room on a quiet street in Hare Town, 2) Hare Town's town square, 3) Iboland forest, and 4) The Great Race course, far outside Hare Town.

Characters (2W, 6M or 4W, 4M):
Mommy Hare: Harriet Hare's mother and Harry Hare's sister.
Harriet Hare: Vivacious, Rudy-of-Cosby-Show like, floppy eared rabbit, niece of Harry Hare.
Harry Hare: Loser of Tortoise and Hare Race, Harriet Hare's uncle, Mommy Hare's brother.
Tommy Tortoise: Winner of Tortoise and Hare Race.
Reporter Tortoise: Television reporter (could be female).
Starter's Voice (Offstage): Offstage Starter of Tortoise and Hare Race.
Ibo Tortoise: Tortoise with shiny, smooth shell.
Skybird: Emissary from Skyland to Ibo Tortoise's forest (could be female).

Moral of the Story

Scene 1

The Scene: Harriet Hare's home living room on a quiet street in
    Hare Town. The set contains a television with a huge
    remote control.

At Rise: It is after school, before dinner. Mommy Hare is
    helping Harriet Hare study her spelling words.

Mommy Hare: Apple.
Harriet Hare: Apple. *(spells)* A P P L E. Apple.
Mommy Hare: Very good.
Harriet Hare: Can I turn the TV on, now?
Mommy Hare: One more word. Button.
Harriet Hare: Button. *(spells)* B U T O N. Button.
Mommy Hare: No, Harriet. Button is spelled with two Ts. Now
    spell it, again.
Harriet Hare: But Mommy! We're going to miss Uncle Harry's
    commercial!
Mommy Hare: Then you'd better hurry.
Harriet Hare: *(very fast)* Button. *(spells)* B U T T O N. Button.
    Now Mommy? Please?!
Mommy Hare: Just one more word, Harriet. Carrot.
Harriet Hare: Oh, Mommy, "everybody" knows how to spell
    carrot! Please, can I turn the TV on?! Please, Mommy,
    please?!
Mommy Hare: Alright. Turn it on. *(Harriet turns the TV on and
    Harry Hare pops up within the television.)*
Harry Hare: Carrots! Can't beat them! Carrots! Know why I eat
    them? They're just bursting with beta-carotene that's so
    good for my skin and fur! Carrot Salad! Carrot Soup.
    Carrot-Raisin Cookies! And my all time favorite, Carrot
    Cake! Carrot sauce over rice is so very nice! Any way you
    fix them, carrots taste as good as they are good for you!
    Eat carrots raw for a snack that

1

Harry Hare *(cont):* can't be beat! Eat them steamed. Eat them boiled. Eat them baked. Eat your carrots for goodness sake! Brought to you by the National Council on Carrots.

(As the commercial ends, Mommy Hare turns off the TV and Harry Hare falls out of sight inside.)

Harriet Hare: Wasn't Uncle Harry great?!
Mommy Hare: I must say, he was pretty good!
Harriet Hare: Pretty good?! Uncle Harry was wonderful! Wonderful. *(spells)* W O N D E R F U L. Wonderful! And famous! Uncle Harry's the most famous rabbit in all the land! Can I call my friends? Can I? Can I, please?!
Mommy Hare: Okay, okay. But just call three.

(Harriet Hare grabs phone as Mommy Hare exits.)

Harriet Hare: Hi Betty Bunny. Did you see him? Did you see my Uncle Harry?

(Lights down. Scene ends.)

Scene 2

The Scene: Hare Town's town square.
The set contains a park bench.

At Rise: It is mid afternoon. Tommy Tortoise and Harry Hare
    are playing checkers. Harry Hare is jumping pieces all over
    the game-board.

Tommy Tortoise: You can't jump in circles.
Harry Hare: Yes, I can. I jump in circles all the time. *(Harry*
    Hare jumps around in a circle.)
Tommy Tortoise: You can't do it playing checkers.
Harry Hare: Why not?
Tommy Tortoise: It's not how the game is played.
Harry Hare: It isn't?
Tommy Tortoise: No, it isn't.
Harry Hare: Says who?
Tommy Tortoise: If you won't play fair, I'm not going to play
    with you.
Harry Hare: You're just jealous 'cause you can't win.
Tommy Tortoise: I could, if you played fair. Besides, winning
    isn't everything.
Harry Hare: Oh, no?! What's better than winning… losing?!
    (Harry Hare mimics running a race.) He's nearing the
    finish line! *(Harry Hare's running slows.)* He's slowing
    down! *(Harry Hare slows to a tortoise pace.)* Yes, folks,
    he's slowing to a mere crawl! *Harry Hare gets on his*
    hands and knees.)
Tommy Tortoise: *(laughs)* You look funny!
Harry Hare: It looks like… Yes! It looks like Harry Hare has lost
    the race! *(Harry Hare jumps up like the winning boxer in*
    the ring, arms raised, jumping up and down.) I lost! I lost!
    Isn't it wonderful? Isn't it simply marvelous that there's
    more to life than winning?! Whoopee! I lost!
Tommy Tortoise: Silly rabbit!
Harry Hare: I'm a hare, not a rabbit. And there nothing more
    important than winning.
Tommy Tortoise: Yes, there is.
Harry Hare: You're sure?
Tommy Tortoise: Yes, I'm sure.

3

Harry Hare: Positively sure?

Tommy Tortoise: Absolutely, positively sure, I am.

Harry Hare: Then why do you care how I win this game of checkers?

Tommy Tortoise: Because you've got to play fair.

Harry Hare: Fair, shmare and a flying bear. Want to race?

Tommy Tortoise: Race? What kind of race?

Harry Hare: The only kind that matters... a footrace!

Tommy Tortoise: Why would I race you?!

Harry Hare: So you can loose, remember?! Isn't loosing everything?

Tommy Tortoise: I didn't say that.

Harry Hare: You said winning isn't everything, didn't you?

Tommy Tortoise: Yes, but-

Harry Hare: Then losing's got to be everything else that winning isn't.

Tommy Tortoise: Did I say that?

Harry Hare: And since I'm going to beat you fair and square...

Tommy Tortoise: Fair and square?

Harry Hare: If you dare.

Tommy Tortoise: And if I win?

Harry Hare: *(laughs)* If you win?! *(Harry Hare puts his arm around Tommy Tortoise's shoulder.)* Don't worry, my cracked-shelled friend. You won't win! Besides, winning isn't everything, remember? *(Harry Hare and Tommy Tortoise start their exit, still together, but Harry Hare has trouble walking so slowly.)*

Harry Hare: Can you move a little faster?

Tommy Tortoise: *(concerned)* Are we racing, now?

Harry Hare: Oh, no! We're not racing now. The whole town needs to see. *(Harry Hare moves behind Tommy Tortoise and starts pushing him off.)* Everybody needs to know just how great it is to lose.

Tommy Tortoise: Everybody?

Harry Hare: Hey! You're not as heavy as you look!

(The pair near their exit.)

Tommy Tortoise: Everybody? You're sure everybody needs to see?

(Harry Hare pushes Tommy Tortoise off. Scene ends.)

Scene 3

The Scene: Harriet Hare's home living room.
The set contains a television with a huge remote control.

At Rise: Harriet Hare is in front of her TV holding the remote
control. Reporter Tortoise is on the Morning News,
microphone in hand.

Reporter Tortoise: But why would Tommy Tortoise race Harry
Hare? *(steps out in front of television)* That's like a robin
racing an eagle. Everybody knows who's going to win.
Everybody knows which one's the fastest. Inquiring minds
already know! Isn't the outcome obvious?

(Tommy Tortoise starts his long, slow entrance during next.)

Harriet Hare: For once Reporter Tortoise is talking sense. Of
course we know who's going to win! My Uncle Harry's
going to win, that's who!
Reporter Tortoise: So then, what's really up with this race?
Inquiring minds want to know. To find out, Tommy Tortoise
has agreed to an exclusive interview before today's Great
Race.

*(Reporter Tortoise moves as slowly as a tortoise to greet
Tommy Tortoise.)*

Reporter Tortoise: Tommy Tortoise, can you tell our viewers
why you agreed to this race, knowing full well that you
cannot win?
Tommy Tortoise: Winning isn't everything.
Reporter Tortoise: But certainly you know… I mean
"everybody" knows rabbits are faster than turtles.
Tommy Tortoise: I am a tortoise, same as you. And Harry's a
hare-
Reporter Tortoise: But I wouldn't race a rabbit-
Tommy Tortoise: I said, Harry Hare is a hare, not a rabbit.
Rabbits are little, itty-bitsy-

6

Reporter Tortoise: Okay! Okay! He's a great big strong hare! All the more reason not to make a fool of yourself by-

Tommy Tortoise: I am not making a fool of myself. Winning isn't everything. It's how you run the race that really matters.

Reporter Tortoise: But certainly you're not saying that-

Tommy Tortoise: I've got to go. *(Tommy Tortoise turns away from the microphone and exits as Reporter Tortoise goes back inside the television during next.)*

Tommy Tortoise: I've got to get to the starting line on time, you know.

Reporter Tortoise: Well there you have it, Folks, in his own words! The race will officially start at 10:00. That's 10:00am... in three hours.

Harriet Hare: Three hours!

Reporter Tortoise: Those of you at work can tune into our sister radio station for the latest update- *(Harriet Hare punches the remote and Reporter Tortoise falls out of sight within the TV.)*

Harriet Hare: I can't bring a radio to school! And they won't let us watch it on TV. Today's The Great Spelling Bee! They'll never postpone The Great Spelling Bee!

Mommy Hare: *(from offstage)* Harriet! Turn that television off and come to breakfast, this moment! You know you need a good breakfast, especially since today's The Great Spelling Bee.

Harriet Hare: I'm not watching TV, Mommy!

Mommy Hare: Don't split hairs with me! And watch that tone of voice, Young Lady!

Harriet Hare: Yes, Ma'am. I'm coming. *(Harriet Hare does not see Mommy Hare enter.)*

Harriet Hare: *(stomping her foot)* Silly grownups!

Mommy Hare: Are you calling me silly?!

Harriet Hare: Oh, no, Mommy! I'd never call you silly! And you'd never put The Great Race smack in the middle of The Great Spelling Bee! Why didn't Uncle Harry ask me, if I could take off school, today? Didn't he know I'd want to be there to see?

Mommy Hare: I know, Sweetheart. I'd like to be there, myself. But we've all got to be where we've all got to be. And we've all got to do what we've all got to do. Now go eat, so you and your brother don't miss your bus.

(Harriet Hare exits and Mommy Hare follows. Scene ends.)

Scene 4

The Scene: The starting line of the Great Race in Hare Town's town square.
The set contains the park bench, starting blocks and the first lap of the race circled with orange cones around the stage.

At Rise: Harry Hare waits most impatiently at the starting line.

Harry Hare: He's going to be late! He's going to be late! He's going to be late for a very important race! What if he's not here when it's time for us to go? What if he's not here when they say, on your mark, get set, go?! I've met rocks that aren't this slow! *(peers offstage)* There he is just creeping along. *(shouts to offstage)* Tommy Tortoise, would you please come on! *(shivers at the sight)* Ooh, it just gives me the creeps to see somebody creeping like that! How did I trick him into racing with me, if he can't move any faster than a tree? *(looks offstage and yawns)* I move faster than that in my sleep! I must talk just as good as I run to trick that slowpoke… *(yawns)* that so slow slowpoke…

(Harry Hare stretches, yawns then lies down, waiting, while Tommy Tortoise enters, exerting every effort to hurry, though he moves as slowly as a tortoise.)

Tommy Tortoise: Did somebody call me? *(Tommy Tortoise slowly sets himself in the starting blocks as Harry Hare dozes.)*
Starter's Voice: *(from offstage)* On your mark! *(beat)* Get set! *(beat)* Go!

(The shot fires and Tommy Tortoise starts on the onstage part of the course. Harry Hare awakens, slowly.)

Harry Hare: What?! What was that?! Did somebody say on your mark, get set, go?! *(looks around)* Oh, that's right. I am in a "very" serious footrace, aren't I? *(Harry Hare mimics Tommy Tortoise's slow, plodding gate and goes to the starting line.)* I'd better hurry, or I might not win! *(laughs)* On my mark! *(Harry Hare squats down at starting line.)* Get set! *(Harry Hare lifts his furry tail to starting position.)* Go! *(Harry Hare bolts into the race, catches and circles the steadily plodding Tommy Tortoise.)*

Harry Hare: Well, Tommy Tortoise, My Good Man, how goes the tortoise race?

Tommy Tortoise: The tortoise race is going fine Harry Hare. How goes the hare race, My Good Man?

Harry Hare: Hare Race?! You are kidding, aren't you, my cracked-shell friend?! *(laughs)* If this were a hare race, then you'd already know that I am going to win! *(laughs)*

(Harry Hare grabs Tommy Tortoise by the arm and twirls him around and around as he circles him.)

Tommy Tortoise: *(laughs)* Whoa! You're making me dizzy, my long-eared Friend! And dizzy's not good… no, not good… not even a little.

(Tommy Tortoise unlooses himself from Harry Hare and sits, holding his head between his hands. Harry Hare continues to circle.)

Tommy Tortoise: Every time I've ever fallen on my back, it took half of Tortoise Town to flip me back over, right-side up! Do you know how long it takes so many tortoises to get to one place?

Harry Hare: Long enough for me to take another nap?

Tommy Tortoise: Long enough to eat some lunch "and" take and nap. *(Harry Hare starts to slow, then has a thought.)*

9

Harry Hare: Oh no you don't! You're not tricking me into taking another nap! You're not tricking me into losing this race!

(Harry Hare circles wider, about to break orbit and finish the race.)

Tommy Tortoise: Trick you?! Who? Me?! Me, Tommy Tortoise, trick the famous Harry Hare, who has been on TV?! Who among all us animals could trick someone as famous as you?

Harry Hare: I am famous, aren't I?

Tommy Tortoise: As famous as carrot cake, carrot sauce and carrot soup!

Harry Hare: Famous… Yep, famous! That's me!

Tommy Tortoise: The fastest hare in all of Hare Town!

Harry Hare: Yep, yep, I'm the fastest… the fastest there is!

Tommy Tortoise: Will you show me how fast you can circle around the slow pokes you race?

Harry Hare: Slow pokes like you? *(Harry Hare moves as fast as he can around Tommy Tortoise.)*

Tommy Tortoise: I'm the slowest and pokiest slow poke there is. Wow! You're really something, Harry the famous hare! I'm so proud to be racing you, I'll tell you a story. That's what I'll do. *(Harry Hare's circling slows with sudden interest in a good story.)*

Harry Hare: Boy, I'm getting nowhere, super fast! Whew! What possible story can you tell to keep this much too slow race from being boring as well?

Tommy Tortoise: A mystery story.

Harry Hare: *(intrigued)* What kind of mystery?

Tommy Tortoise: A famous mystery for a famous hare. Once upon a time, tortoise and turtle shells were smooth and shiny like snails' shells and clams' shells… as shiny as an oyster's pearl.

Harry Hare: Oh, that's silly! Everybody knows tortoises have always had cracks in your shells! Now I've got to finish this race!

Tommy Tortoise: It was at the Great Picnic in Skyland where our shells got these cracks all over our backs-

10

Harry Hare: The Great Picnic, where?!

Tommy Tortoise: In Skyland. You know… Skyland? *(beat)* You've never heard of Skyland?!

Harry Hare: I've heard of rabbit holes and Wonderland.

Tommy Tortoise: Well Skyland is higher up than Wonderland is down! Only the strongest birds fly as high as Skyland is high!

Harry Hare: Never heard of it!

Tommy Tortoise: Oh, then let me tell you quick, so you won't be so ignorant!

Harry Hare: Ignorant?! Are you calling me ignorant-?!

Tommy Tortoise: Hush and listen! Listen and hush! Once upon a time in the land of the Ibo *(pronounced: eeboe),* tortoises were the most beautiful animals in the forest. Our shells were smooth and shiny like an oyster's pearl. We were, without a doubt, the most important and absolutely most beautiful animals in all the world!

Harry Hare: Oh! You're going to tell me how you tortoises got to be so ugly? How'd it happen?! Go on with your story! Do go on!

Tommy Tortoise: How we got to be so ugly? Humph. Very funny. But as I was saying, once upon a time in the land of the Ibo, tortoises were the most beautiful animals in all the forest. Our shells were smooth and shiny like an oyster's pearl. But when Ibo Tortoise proclaimed himself the leader of all, the animals rebelled from the great to the small. They said, "No! Ibo Tortoise will never lead us!" Then they left him alone, and wouldn't listen to him fuss.

Harry Hare: Well go on, Tommy Tortoise! What happened next?

Tommy Tortoise: That's when Skybird came.

Harry Hare: Who?

(Harry Hare continues circling as he and Tommy Tortoise exit. Scene ends.)

Scene 5

The Scene: Iboland forest.
The set contains trees growing among boulders.

At Rise: Ibo Tortoise sits on a boulder admiring his smooth,
    shiny shell. Skybird enters and listens to the monologue,
    unnoticed.

Ibo Tortoise: Who's the handsomest tortoise in all these parts?
    The animals' leader in beauty and smarts? I should be the
    forest leader, in sooth and in truth. Everyone would bring
    me food, like rabbit's tasty orange roots. We'd all sing and
    dance from ground to forest roof. But they don't think much
    of leaders here. They don't care that I'm very good at
    leading to the far and near—
Skybird: *(to himself)* Did he say, leader? *(Skybird flutters to Ibo
    Tortoise.)* Did you say that you're the leader down here?
Ibo Tortoise: *(looks around)* Down where?
Skybird: Here. Down here out of the sky. I've come to invite you
    to our feast up there, *(points)* up there high.
Ibo Tortoise: A feast?! To a feast?! A feast up there, where?!
Skybird: Not just you. I'm here to invite you and all those you
    lead to join us in Skyland for a Great Feast, indeed. *(beat)*
    You are the leader here, right? I was sent to speak to the
    leader, only.
Ibo Tortoise: The leader, here? Oh, yes, indeed… yes, indeed!
    I will lead the Forest Creatures to your Great Feast. But if
    Skyland is truly where you live, only the birds can eat what
    you give.
Skybird: Only birds? But why? Are all the rest of you afraid to
    fly?
Ibo Tortoise: Afraid to fly? Oh, no. Not I. I am not afraid to fly.
    Only…
Skybird: Only what?
Ibo Tortoise: Only I cannot fly. I don't know how. Never learned.
Skybird: Never?!
Ibo Tortoise: Never.
Skybird: Are there many like you?

12

Ibo Tortoise: Only birds fly, down here.

Skybird: Only birds?!

Ibo Tortoise: Well, butterflies, moths and insect, galore. And
 bats, of course, and some strange looking squirrels... and
 even stranger fish-

Skybird: Fish? What's a fish?

Ibo Tortoise: They live in the ocean.

Skybird: And fly?! Oh, my! We have no oceans up in the sky!
 Skyland's no place for fish who can fly. I think they would
 die in our land in the sky. It's too dry, much too dry for fish
 who fly.

Ibo Tortoise: Then we'll leave them here-

Skybird: Good. Good. The sky's much too dry for fish who fly.

Ibo Tortoise: And too high *(tries to jump)* for us who can't fly.
 (Skybird plucks the longest feather from his tail.)

Skybird: Ow! *(Skybird hands the feather to Ibo Tortoise.)*

Skybird: Ow, that smarts! Here, take my magic tail feather.
 Then, when everyone's all gathered together, hold hands
 and hold up this feather. It will carry you all up high through
 the sky. And then, when we're all done feasting, it will bring
 you back home for digesting and sleeping.

Ibo Tortoise: This feather can carry us all at one time?

Skybird: Absolutely! Absolutely all, it will. Just hold hands real
 tight and come one and all to eat your fill. Eat your fill. Eat
 your fill. *(Skybird exits, rubbing the place where his feather
 had been.)*

Ibo Tortoise: Eat to my fill. Oh yes I will. I will eat to my fill.
 Everybody! Everybody, come and hear! We're going to a
 feast- *(Suddenly Ibo Tortoise slaps his hands to his
 mouth.)* Shh, silly tortoise! So much food and drink...
 Hmm... I am the leader, no matter what the rest of them
 think. The leader decides what the people will do. I'll bring
 food back to them. I'll make a nice stew of the leftover
 foods from Skyland's Great Feast. I'll just fly up there "for"
 them and be back in a wink. *(Ibo Tortoise takes the magic
 feather and twirls 'round and 'round as the lights change
 and the winds blow.)* Skyland here I come!

(Ibo Tortoise exits. Scene ends.)

Scene 6

The Scene: The Great Race course, far outside Hare Town.
The set is identical to Iboland forest of Scene 6 with the
    addition of orange cones that mark the course of the race.

At Rise: Tommy Tortoise enters with Harry Hare circling him.
    Harry Hare is obviously very tired but is fixed on Tommy
    Tortoise's story.

Harry Hare: But what if Ibo Tortoise got lost? He'd never been
    to Skyland, before. He'd never flown before!
Tommy Tortoise: Maybe he was as smart and strong as you.
Harry Hare: As smart and strong as I am?!
Tommy Tortoise: Well just look at you! You've been circling me
    for miles and miles!
Harry Hare: So?
Tommy Tortoise: Don't you see? You've run ten times ten more
    miles than me. And just look at you! You don't even need
    to rest. I surely do. Yes sirree I do. Why don't you?
    (Tommy Tortoise stops moving and Harry Hare slows his
    circling to a very tired walk.)
Harry Hare: Maybe *(huffs and puffs)* I could use a teensy tiny
    rest-
Tommy Tortoise: You don't need to rest because you are the
    strongest, the strongest there is. I sure wish I was as
    strong as you. Then I could finish the story and keep
    running, too.
Harry Hare: Maybe a rest would do us both some good-
Tommy Tortoise: Oh no, no. I couldn't ask you to wait here with
    me.
Harry Hare: I'll just wait *(huffs and puffs)* while you finish the
    Ibo Tortoise story.
Tommy Tortoise: It's really that good?!
Harry Hare: It will be when you get to the ugly part.
Tommy Tortoise: The ugly part?

Harry Hare: You know. The "How You Got Your Cracks And Bumps And Ridges" part.

Tommy Tortoise: Oh, that part. Okay.

Harry Hare: And the "How He Could Carry So Much Food Back By Himself" part. *(Tommy Tortoise and Harry Hare sit.)*

Harry Hare: A sack so big and full enough to feed the whole forest seems much too heavy for one flying tortoise to hold.

Tommy Tortoise: But that was something Ibo Tortoise didn't know. Feather in one hand, this huge sack in the other, Ibo Tortoise stepped off Skyland and floated and gloated and floated some more... *(Harry Hare yawns.)* Am I boring you? I'm so sorry. Please feel free to go.

Harry Hare: Oh, no, please continue. I'll just rest my eyes, while I listen.

Tommy Tortoise: Are you sure?

Harry Hare: I said, go on. Finish the story right now or I'll go!

Tommy Tortoise: Ibo Tortoise gloated and floated and gloated some more... Then it happened!

Harry Hare: Then what *(yawns)* happened?

Tommy Tortoise: The sack started slipping. Right through his fingers, it slid. It was slipping away, so you know what he did? *(beat)* I said, do you know what he did?

Harry Hare: Just tell the story, would you? *(yawns)* You're messing with the flow!

Tommy Tortoise: Ibo Tortoise grabbed the sack with both hands and dropped the feather... You're falling asleep, Harry Hare!

Harry Hare: No I'm not!

Tommy Tortoise: Yes, you are! *(Tommy Tortoise stands.)* Get up, Harry Hare. Get up to your feet or I will stop telling this story. Oh yes I will and you will be sorry!

Harry Hare: Can't I just lie here and listen?

Tommy Tortoise: Oh, no! No way. No, not today! *(Tommy Tortoise pulls Harry Hare to his feet.)* The second that feather fell from his hand, Ibo Tortoise came crashing down into the rocks all over the land. *(Tommy Tortoise starts spinning and twirling as though he were falling.)*

Tommy Tortoise: Kerplum! Bumpity, bump, bump, boom!

15

(Tommy Tortoise falls and accidentally lands on his back with his feet and arms sticking up.) Oops!

Harry Hare: *(laughs)* Look at you! Look at you! I'll bet that's exactly how Ibo Tortoise looked!

(Harry Hare reenacts Tommy Tortoise falling.)

Harry Hare: Kerplum! Bumpity, bump, bump, boom!

(Harry Hare rocks to his back and sticks his feet up in the air.)

Harry Hare: *(drawls)* Oo-oops!

(Harry Hare is consumed with laughter while Tommy Tortoise rocks back and forth, trying to get up.)

Tommy Tortoise: Very funny. Will you help me up?
Harry Hare: *(laughing)* Oh, my sides hurt!
Tommy Tortoise: Then stop laughing so much and, please, help me up. I'm getting seasick, rocking like this.
Harry Hare: Then stop rocking and finish the story, 'cause I am not calling Tortoise Town to come flip you over.
Tommy Tortoise: What do you think there is to tell? He fell to the ground and broke his shell. Now, please, help me up! Seasick's not good. Worse than dizzy, it is. *(Harry Hare leans over and stops Tommy Tortoise's rocking.)*
Harry Hare: Do go on.
Tommy Tortoise: From here?! From here on my back?! I don't believe you would treat me like that!

(Harry Hare yawns, stretches, settles down comfortably beside Tommy Tortoise and closes his eyes.)

Tommy Tortoise: Okay! Okay I'll finish the tale. So this great big Ibo Tortoise and all the leftovers from the Great Feast, crashed down on the rockiest, stoniest, hardest part of the forest. The end! Now, please, help me up so we can finish this race-!

Harry Hare: Can't be.

Tommy Tortoise: Can't be what?

Harry Hare: Can't be the end. Wake me up, when you're ready
to tell the real ending, my cracked-shell Friend.

Tommy Tortoise: Wake you?! Harry Hare, don't you dare-!
*(Harry Hare snores, loudly. Tommy Tortoise watches him,
intently, then starts singing, softly, to the "Rock A Bye
Baby" melody.)* Rock a bye, Harry. Dream of Skyland.
While the hare snores, Tommy Tortoise will
stand...*(Tommy Tortoise rocks back and forth.)*

Tommy Tortoise: When I rock up and onto my feet...*(Tommy
Tortoise rocks onto his feet.)* Tommy Tortoise: I'll beat
Harry Hare, who lies snoring, asleep.

*(Tommy Tortoise exits slowly, quietly chuckling. Lights down on
Harry Hare, snoring quite comfortably. Scene ends.)*

Scene 7

The Scene: Harriet Hare's home living room.
The set contains a television and huge remote control.

At Rise: Harriet Hare punches the TV's remote control.
     Reporter Tortoise pops up.)

Reporter Tortoise: And now The Afternoon News for my Floppy
     Eared Friends!
Harriet Hare: How'd you know my ears are floppy? They could
     be invisible like yours… if tortoises even "have" ears.
Reporter Tortoise: The price of carrots continues to fall. Even
     rabbits have stopped eating their carrots, since Harry Hare
     lost the Great Race.
Harriet Hare: He lost?! Uncle Harry lost?! Mommy!
Reporter Tortoise: On a happier note, sweet-potatoes are
     making a comeback! *(Harriet Hare punches the remote
     and Reporter Tortoise falls out of sight inside the TV.)*
Harriet Hare: Who cares about sweet-potatoes or carrots?!
     Uncle Harry lost! (throws head back and shouts) Mommy!
     (Mommy Hare enters.)
Mommy Hare: Harriet Hare, if you don't stop that caterwauling-!
Harriet Hare: Uncle Harry lost, Mommy! He lost the footrace!
Mommy Hare: Who told you that? Your brother? He was just
     teasing you, Honey—
Harriet Hare: It wasn't Dopey… I mean Joey. It was on TV,
     Mommy. "Everybody" knows about Uncle Harry "except"
     us, Mommy! I won't be able to hold my ears up anywhere.
Mommy Hare: As long as your uncle did his best… *(A timer
     beeps from the kitchen.)* We'll all hold our ears up, just
     fine. It was just a footrace, right?

(Mommy Hare exits.)

Harriet Hare: "Just" a footrace?! A footrace lost to a tortoise
     isn't "just" a footrace! Lost to a tortoise! A skinny little lizard
     stuck inside a big, heavy, ugly, cracked shell! How could
     "my" Uncle Harry lose to somebody as slow as that? *(beat)*

18

Uncle Harry can beat any tortoise in the land… with his hands tied behind him.

(Harriet Hare doesn't notice Harry Hare enter, racing across stage with both hands tied behind him and exit.)

Harriet Hare: And his feet tied together.

(Harry Hare enters, hopping across stage with his feet tied together and exits.)

Harriet Hare: My Uncle Harry could've beat a whole herd of galloping tortoises, wearing a blindfold!

(Harry Hare enters blindfolded, hops across stage with his hands and feet tied and sits down, tired and dejected.)

Harriet Hare: My Uncle Harry has the fastest feet in all the land.

(Harriet Hare turns to Harry Hare.)

Harriet Hare: Don't you, Uncle Harry? Don't you have the fastest feet in all the land?
Harry Hare: Yes… yes, I do. The fastest two. *(Harry Hare wiggles out of his bindings and takes off his blindfold.)*
Harriet Hare: My uncle can run circles around any tortoise in the land.
Harry Hare: Yes, I could. In fact, yes, I did. I ran circles and circles and circled some more.
Harriet Hare: Does Mommy know you're here?
Harry Hare: No. Not yet. How was your spelling bee?
Harriet Hare: How was your race? *(Mommy Hare steps just inside the room.)*
Harry Hare: I lost. I fell asleep.
Harriet Hare: Fell asleep?! That was the best that you could do? Fall asleep?!
Mommy Hare: Watch your tone, young Lady!
Harriet Hare: But Mommy! He went to sleep. Went to sleep!
Mommy Hare: Is that true, Harry?

Harry Hare: He tricked me. Tommy Tortoise tricked me!

Mommy Hare: Sounds to me like you tricked yourself, unless he knocked you down and tied you up.

Harry Hare: Nobody knocked me down, Sis. Nobody tied me up.

Mommy Hare: I didn't think so. Seems like both of you gave yourselves a bad day. Isn't that right, Harriet Hare? *(beat)* Tell your uncle how The Great Spelling Bee went. *(Harriet Hare pouts and turns away.)* Young Lady, please don't turn away from me, when I'm talking to you.

Harriet Hare: Yes, Ma'am. I lost The Great Spelling Bee, Uncle Harry, same as you.

Harry Hare: That can't be true! Not someone as smart as you! They must have tricked you with some word too hard and too long for a second grader to do-

Mommy Hare: Harry Hare, did excuses work for you? *(to Harriet Hare)* Tell your uncle the word you missed. *(Harriet Hare mumbles under her breath.)* This time, say it like you want one. Go on.

Harriet Hare: Carrot.

Harry Hare: Carrot?! You missed spelling carrot?! How could you misspell carrot?!

Mommy Hare: The same way you fell asleep. Too cocky. Too sure of yourselves. Too disrespectful of others. Too-

Harry Hare: Okay! Okay! We get it. We hear you loud and clear, don't we, Niece?

Harriet Hare: I guess so.

Mommy Hare & Harry Hare: *(together)* You guess so?!

Harriet Hare: I mean, yes, Ma'am. Yes, Uncle Harry. I get it.

Mommy Hare: Good. Good for both of you. I'm going to finish our supper. Why don't the two of you relax for a while? Play some checkers or watch some TV and remember how to smile.

Harry Hare: Can we do all three?

(Harry Hare nudges Harriet Hare conspiratorially.)

Mommy Hare: Will you help her memorize her multiplication tables, when dinner's done?

20

Harry Hare: Absolutely!

(Mommy Hare exits. Harry Hare tries, unsuccessfully to turn on the TV, while Harriet Hare gets her checkers.)

Harriet Hare: I know almost all of my three times tables.
Harry Hare: Almost all?!
Harriet Hare: Almost.
Harry Hare: Let me hear one.
Harriet Hare: Three times six is eighteen!
Harry Hare: Wow! I really do have the smartest niece in all Hare Town!
Harriet Hare: And I've got the best uncle, too! *(Harry Hare and Harriet Hare hug. Harriet Hare takes the control and turns on the TV. Tommy Tortoise pops up within the screen.)*
Tommy Tortoise: Even Ibo Tortoise's wife was angry with him. And he looked really weird without his shell.
Harry Hare: When did Tommy Tortoise get on TV?!
Tommy Tortoise: Ibo Tortoise felt weird, too. And very, very cold! But every time his wife looked at the Great Feast from Skyland, scattered like garbage all over the land, she'd get so angry her heart turned as cold as Ibo Tortoise felt without his shell. "You're the only one who got to eat! Now only vultures and jackals will eat after you! You ought to be cold! You ought to stay cold, too!" she said. Two days passed. Then Ibo Tortoise started sneezing *(sneezes)* and wheezing *(wheezes)* and hacking *(hacks)* and coughing *(coughs)* so much…

(Tommy Tortoise sneezes, wheezes, hacks and coughs, uncontrollably.)

Tommy Tortoise: That his wife stopped being angry and patched up his shell with everything she found that was sticky and hardened well. And ever since that day, every tortoise everywhere has learned Ibo Tortoise's lesson. And we have learned it, very, very well. His lumps and bumps and ridges are on all our shells. Our shells remind us not to

21

be greedy and to share our good fortunes with everyone, everywhere.

Harry Hare: So that's how it ended!

Tommy Tortoise: And now a word from our sponsor.

Harriet Hare: That's how what ended?

Harry Hare: Shh! I'll tell you, later. My commercial's coming on.

(Tommy Tortoise holds up a bunch of carrots.)

Tommy Tortoise: Carrots! Can't beat them! Carrots! Know why I eat them? They're just bursting with beta-carotene that's so good for our skin and our shells! Carrot Salad! Carrot Soup. Carrot-Raisin Cookies! And my all time favorite, Carrot Cake! Carrot sauce over rice is so very nice! Any way you fix them, carrots taste as good as they are good for you! Eat carrots raw for a snack that can't be beat! Eat them steamed. Eat them boiled. Eat them baked. Eat your carrots for goodness sake! Brought to you by the National Council on Carrots.

Harry Hare: They pulled my commercial?! They pulled my commercial and gave it to him?! To him?! Is there no end to the misery! *(beat)* Am I overreacting?

Harriet Hare: Maybe… just a little. (Harriett Hare turn off the TV as Mommy Hare sticks her head through the door.)

Mommy Hare: And over acting, maybe just a lot. But guess what I've got cooling in the window. *(beat)* Give up? *(beat)* An old fashioned carrot pie, just like our mother used to make.

Harriet Hare: Carrot pie?!

Harry Hare: With raisins?

Mommy Hare: With raisins.

(Mommy Hare exits as lights fade.)

Harriet Hare: And coconut?

Mommy Hare: *(from offstage)* Come see for yourselves.

(Harry Hare and Harriet Hare race each other offstage. Lights down. Scene ends. End of play)

The Hare & the Tortoise

A Hare was making fun of the Tortoise one day for being so slow.

"Do you ever get anywhere?" he asked with a mocking laugh.

"Yes," replied the Tortoise, "and I get there sooner than you think. I'll run you a race and prove it."

The Hare was much amused at the idea of running a race with the Tortoise, but for the fun of the thing he agreed. So the Fox, who had consented to act as judge, marked the distance and started the runners off.

The Hare was soon far out of sight, and to make the Tortoise feel very deeply how ridiculous it was for him to try a race with a Hare, he lay down beside the course to take a nap until the Tortoise should catch up.

The Tortoise meanwhile kept going slowly but steadily, and, after a time, passed the place where the Hare was sleeping. But the Hare slept on very peacefully; and when at last he did wake up, the Tortoise was near the goal. The Hare now ran his swiftest, but he could not overtake the Tortoise in time.

The race is not always to the swift.

From Library of Congress, Words to the Wise:
https://read.gov/aesop/index.htm

A similar fable, included by Achebe in his novel "Things Fall Apart" involved a tortoise in a very different guise:

Once the birds were preparing to fly to a great and joyous feast. The tortoise, who was hungry, asked the birds if he could also attend. Although they distrusted the sweet-talking tortoise, they gave him wings and allowed him to fly with them to the banquet. Once there, he anointed himself as the king, and named himself, *"All of you."*

When the host said, "This food is for all of you," he ate most of it and left only scraps for the rest of the birds. They were so angry that they took his feathers away, fly him over his home and dropped him on the ground—thus cracking his shell. This mythological interpretation serves two purposes for the natives: to inform their understanding of why the tortoise has a rough and cracked body; and as a symbol that the greedy missionaries sweet-talked them and stole the richest parts of their culture and traditions.

There is a similar Nigerian version of this same legend:

How The Tortoise Got The Cracks On His Shell

Once upon a time in the animal kingdom, there was a famine. The animals in the kingdom all starved and looked very lean except the birds.

When the Tortoise noticed this, he decided to find out from the birds where they got their food.

The birds refused, citing the Tortoise's cunning as a reason why they wouldn't disclose it.

The Tortoise continued to plead and promised not to play any tricks. The birds then agreed to tell him.

They told him of a feast held high up in the heavens for anyone who could make it up there.

The Tortoise thought about it and realized that it would be impossible for him to get to the heavens because he had no wings. However, an idea struck him; he said, "if only each of you would lend me a feather to attach to my body which would serve as a wing."

The birds agreed and gave him a feather to attach to his body to form wings.

Before they left, the birds asked him to take a ceremonial name, one which he would be addressed by when he got to the heavens.

After thinking about it, the Tortoise said he should be called "Everyone of you," and so they left for the feast.

When they arrived, they were welcomed by the host of heaven and led to the table where a banquet was prepared. "This food is for everyone of you," said the host before leaving.

At that point, the Tortoise stepped forward and reminded them that his ceremonial name was "Everyone of you" and, as such, the food belonged to him alone.

He then went ahead to eat the entire food. When he was done, his smooth shell shone brightly.

The birds were very angry with him and they all agreed to take back their feathers, leaving him with no wings.

The Tortoise, however, pleaded with one of the birds to take a message home for him. "Tell my wife to bring out the softest materials, the beds and the pillows in my house, and put them out under the heavens, so that I can land safely when I jump down."

The bird agreed to take the message, but when he got to the house of the Tortoise, he changed the message. "Your husband has instructed that you bring out the strong and hard materials in the house out in the open," he said.

27

When the Tortoise saw his wife bringing out materials, he became assured that he would be able to land safely.

When she had finished, the Tortoise leapt from the heavens, and crashed into the hard materials. His smooth shell shattered into several pieces.

It took the best healer in the land to put his shell together. Thus, until this day, the Tortoise has a broken shell as a reminder of what his greed cost him.

www.ingramcontent.com/pod-product-compliance
Lightning Source LLC
LaVergne TN
LVHW021549080426
835509LV00019B/2924